Prophetic Foundations

Restoration of Purity

APOSTLE SONYA L. THOMPSON

ISBN: 9798733150352

Prophetic Foundation – Restoration of Purity

First Printing

Printed and bound in the United States of America

INTRO

The body of Christ is an hour of reformation. Many systems are being brought back to their original intent and for this to happen, a reformation must take place. One of the areas the Holy Spirit refuses to let go untouched is the office of the prophet. I was in prayer one morning 2020, and the Holy Spirit began to press upon my heart His desire to see a cleansing, reformation, and restoration of purity in the body of Christ as it pertains to the office of the prophet and the body of Christ as a prophetic people. I soon realized our precious Holy Spirit wanted me to have a part in what he was doing. Through my ministry, ARISE Ministries International, as directed by the Lord, we began a School of the Prophets.

The Holy Spirit gave us a different approach for this assignment. Rather than starting with an unveiling of the prophet and the office etc. I was instructed to start from a place of purifying, to begin cleaning the foundation so there would be a pure prophetic flow from those God has assigned to my life and ministry in this hour. This Apostolic Prophetic Manual will impact the lives of thousands because these truths will be handed off to generations.

New Testament prophets & prophetic people need to know who they are and how they are supposed to function in the dispensation we have entered in. We have stepped onto the timeline where the Glorious Church as spoken of in Ephesians 5, is arising! We have been stuck in an Old Testament view and function for way to long. Our limited view, unbiblical practices and mindsets which have crept into the body are being purged as He reforms and restores us to function with greater purity and power in the earth and carry forth this mandate.

May the fruit of this writing be evidenced by an awakening, repentance, and restoration in the lives of everyone who names the name of Christ.

TABLE OF CONTENTS

CHAPTER 1

THE NEED FOR PURITY

It was during a morning prayer time that the Holy Spirit began to share His heart with me concerning the lack of purity in the prophetic office. I began to understand, the heart of God in this hour is to see a massive soul cleansing of the prophets and His prophetic people. That morning I could sense the overwhelming weight of His desire and soon began to realize I had a part to play in this mandate through ARISE Ministries International. The Holy Spirit placed upon my heart to begin an ARISE School of the Prophets. This writing is reflective of our very first few meetings together. We started from the back office so to speak because the Holy Spirit wanted a clean-up before laying a proper foundation.

Even though I am a prophet, and have trained prophets, I did not ever believe this was an area I would teach in. But I have come to realize, our great God will use whoever will listen and obey. He also ensures the individual is equipped to fulfill the mandate at hand. Of course, I could not refuse the invitation! What an honor and privilege to be a part of the reformation and purifying process that is going forth in the prophetic office in this hour!

Whether you are called to the office of the prophet or are a prophetic person, which we all are because the Holy Spirit lives in us, a pure vessel is necessary in order to effectively facilitate the work of the Holy Spirit. It would be difficult to adhere to the task unless we can identify what we are being called back to.

Let's have a look at Psalm 24 as we begin laying a foundation of purity.

Psalm 24:3-4

3 Who may ascend into the hill of the Lord? Or who may stand in His holy place? 4 He who has clean hands and a pure heart, Who has not lifted up his soul to an idol, Nor sworn deceitfully.

The Journey To Purity

David asked a question in the text above. ***"Who may ascend into the hill of the Lord?"*** I can almost see David looking at or meditating on the beautiful presence of Mount Zion, when suddenly this prophetic song begins to flow from the very heart of God. It is a song that asked, how can I ascend, or go and meet with God, visit with Him, and depart with something tangible and substantial for myself and for others? His next verse in the song pushes us even further; ***"Or who may stand in his holy place?"*** David wants to know, when I find this higher position, as I embark on this journey to purity, how do I stand in it? How do I maintain myself on this spiritual platform? What will it take for me to operate seamlessly between these two realms to carry forth this prophetic mandate in the earth? The answer to the question is very clear, and one that cannot be avoided or dismissed if we are to fulfill the desire of the Holy Spirit. We will begin to dissect this journey in the next few chapters.

CHAPTER 2

HE IS INSPECTING OUR HANDS

As we move forward, we begin to see a picture of purity. The one who has clean hands and a pure heart, the one who has not lifted his soul to an idol nor sworn deceitfully, will occupy a place in the face of God that will shift regions, territories, generations, and atmospheres! To have clean hands denotes __innocence__, __blamelessness, emptiness of self__ and one who is __acquitted__ of selfish desires. We know that we can only have this posture when we have fully yielded our lives to Christ. We maintain it by our continuous submission to His Spirit and to His Word.

The Holy Spirit gave me an incredible visual years ago. He showed me what it looks like when we transfer the spot of impurity to the lives of others. Imagine for a moment submerging your hands into a bucket of ashes which cannot be washed off by natural means and you continue to go forth touching a row of beautiful white garments. What do you think will happen? Your dirty hands will leave a lasting impression or spot on everything touched. They will know **<u>YOU</u>** were there. I do not want to leave my touch; I want to leave the touch of God on the lives of everyone I encounter! When God touches us through others, there is only purity and wholeness. This is also what happens when we operate with unclean hands in the realm of the spirit. Whatever our area of error is, we begin to stain everything we touch! In this case, we are talking about functioning prophetically. Because there is error or impurity in this area, the stain continues and has grown at a level and pace which has commanded the attention of the Holy Spirit! What a weighty responsibility we have, to ensure that our hands are not the ones which carry the stain of impurity to taints the garments of God's people. Therefore, we must be a people of purity, a people of clean hands.

The Cost Of Clean Hands

Clean hands are a foundational must for handling the things of God. If we keep this posture our generations will be a people who know of God and His ways. Clean hands require a death of will and total yielding of it to God. Clean hands are indicative of a man or woman of God who refuses to have them dirtied with offense, a sinful/compromising lifestyle or become insensitive to the drawing of the Holy Spirit when he calls them to a place of repentance. Clean hands do not use profanity and make excuses for it. As a matter of fact, an individual with clean hands never compromises to justify their sin! Clean hands do not rob God or hold back material things because of covetousness, greed, and fear. A person with clean hands tithes, gives and is a blessing to others. Surely you must know all of these things matter to God!

The Holy Spirit is in the process of inspecting our hands. We can no longer be ignorant and immature, touching what is holy as if it were common. We can no longer casually touch the glory of God in an ordinary and sloppy manner. We can no longer expect to operate at full capacity and continue to dishonor the requirements of a holy God. Prophet, are your hands clean? Prophetic people, are your hands clean? How dare we continue to tell the Lord we want to do His will and give ourselves away to Him if we continue to disobey the foundations of Christianity. Clean hands are NOT an option, they are an expectation.

The Cost Of Unclean Hands

We get a picture of this in 2 Samuel Chapter 6, when David began to move the ark of the covenant. In this account, Uzzah was killed for touching the ark as he tried to steady it on the cart.

2 Samuel 6:6-8

6 And when they came to Nachon's threshing floor, Uzzah put out his hand to the ark of God and took hold of it, for the oxen stumbled. 7 Then the anger of the Lord was aroused against Uzzah, and God struck him there for his error; and he died there by the ark of God. 8 And David became angry because of the Lord's outbreak against Uzzah; and he called the name of the place Perez Uzzah to this day.

The Bible says that day, David became afraid of God! A study of Scripture reveals the priests were designated to carry the ark by poles, not on a cart. After reading this account, the thought of touching the things of God in an impure state should invoke great fear in our lives. I believe we do not have this fear in us because teaching on the love and grace of God have been used as a means to slip in an out of sin. But one thing I am confident of, the Holy Spirit is at the height of tolerance in this area.

Prophet of the Lord, prophetic people of God, we are being called to a higher place in Christ Jesus. We are being summoned by the Holy Spirit to return to a place where our hands are clean. A place where we adhere to the protocols of God and stop saying, "Well God knows my heart. He knows what I mean." Yes, He does know your heart, that is why He is calling us back to a place of cleanliness! The Lord is no longer overlooking our ignorance. We have come to a place in this decade and dispensation where we shall be required to come up to the standard of the Holy Spirit and handle the "ark" properly. Anything less than this will no longer be tolerated!

Acts 17:29-31

29 Therefore, since we are the offspring of God, we ought not to think that the Divine Nature is like gold or silver or stone, something shaped by art and man's devising. 30 <u>Truly, these times of ignorance God overlooked, but now commands all men everywhere to repent,</u> 31 because He has appointed a day on *which He will judge the world in righteous-ness by the Man whom He has ordained. He has given assurance of this to all by raising Him from the dead."*

The things He overlooked in the past will no longer be overlooked in this present age. God is calling His prophets and prophetic people to a place of repentance. He wants us to look at our hands and survey if we are in fact in a position to touch and handle what we say we are ready for!

CHAPTER 3

I NEED A PURE HEART

As we continue through Psalm 24, David's song also says we need a **PURE** heart to stay in this high place and on the holy hill. We need a pure heart to accommodate our clean hands. Again, we must ask the question of what a pure heart is to God. A pure heart is a heart empty of selfish desires, devoid of selfish ambition or recognition. A pure heart is a heart possessed by an individual who has permitted the Word of God to purge them of the traditions of men and the idols of this world. A pure heart is a heart that's fixed trusting in the Lord as indicated in **Psalm 112**.

If we are ever in doubt of what our Father's expectations are of us, we have One to look at, the prototype — Jesus Christ who will never leave us in doubt.

Hebrews 11:1-3

1 God, who at various times and in various ways spoke in time past to the fathers by the *prophets, 2 has in these last days spoken to us by His Son, whom He has appointed heir of all things, through whom also He made the worlds; 3 <u>who being the brightness of His glory and the express image of His person,</u> and upholding all things by the word of His power, when He had by Himself purged our sins, sat down at the right hand of the Majesty on high,*

Whenever we are in doubt or use the common phrase "What this looks like," we can always look to Jesus the author and finisher of our faith. He is our real-life expression of how we ought to walk as prophets and prophetic people.

I can of Myself do nothing. As I hear, I judge; and My judgment is righteous, because I do not seek My own will but the will of the Father who sent Me. (John 5:30)

Then Jesus answered and said to them, "Most assuredly, I say to you, the Son can do nothing of Himself, but what He sees the Father do; for whatever He does, the Son also does in like manner (John 5:19).

Jesus did not **DO** anything He did not see the Father doing. He also did not **SAY** anything the Father was not saying. This is the posture of a prophet!

> ***Jesus said to them, "If God were your Father, you would love Me, for I proceeded forth and came from God; nor have I come of Myself, but He sent Me." (John 8:42)***

We have no excuse of not knowing what is expected of us. It is very simple; just say and do what the Father is doing. We talk when we are spoken to and when He is silent, so are we!

Clean hands and a pure heart are the essential elements to the restoration of this great prophetic calling. We cannot bypass this requirement, nor will the Lord allow us to do so either, because we have a great call of ushering in Glorious Church in this decade

I decree and declare as you proceed through this book, you will sense an awakening and awareness to this call. May the fear of the Living God begin to burn like a fire within you, and may His anointing be released upon you to function on a level of accuracy and purity you have yet to know!

CHAPTER 4

HINDERANCES TO PURITY

I do not believe there is anyone who does not desire to live a clean and pure life before the Lord and His people, but many have fallen short. If we are going to say, "Thus says the Lord," we better make sure we have an environment which is prepared to accommodate His word. Are you preparing a place for Him? The Word of God requires a clean and pure vessel to flow through if it is going to have a purest and most powerful impact. The religious mindset will think I am talking about perfection. I am not talking about being perfect because our perfection is in Christ Jesus. However, I am talking about a people who WILLINGLY participate in what they know to be sin or make compromises for doing so! We like to take our willful sin and hide behind the guise of, "I know I am not perfect." That is a conversation of the flesh when an out for sin is being looked for.

So, let us look at some of the things which will hinder our vessels from being a pure environment. We are going to take a moment and survey the gates of our lives.

<u>FAILURE TO GUARD THE GATES</u>

In the Old Testament there is great discussion about the temple and its gates. I loved one account found in the book of Ezra. In this account, the beginning of restoration of the **temple** required that the word of the Prophet Jeremiah be brought forth into their present age.

> ***1 Now in the first year of Cyrus king of Persia, that the word of the Lord by the mouth of Jeremiah might be fulfilled, the Lord stirred up the spirit of Cyrus king of Persia, so that he made a proclamation throughout all his kingdom, and also put it in writing, saying, 2 Thus says Cyrus king of Persia: All the kingdoms of the earth the Lord God of heaven has given me. And He has commanded me to build Him a house at Jerusalem which is in Judah. 3 Who is among you of all His people? May his God be with him, and let him go up to Jerusalem which is in Judah, and build the house of the Lord God of Israel (He is God), which is in Jerusalem. 4 And whoever is left***

in any place where he dwells, let the men of his place help him with silver and gold, with goods and livestock, besides the freewill offerings for the house of God which is in Jerusalem.

(Ezra 1:1-4)

It was for this reason that the Lord stirred up the spirit of Cyrus the King of Persia. He was about to use him mightily as a conduit and a partaker in the fulfillment of the word Jeremiah had declared (see ***Jeremiah 29***). I believe even now, there is a word of purity that has caught up with the body of Christ, and the Lord has stirred up His prophets, the remnant, to prophetically call us back to the foundations, and to purity because we have allowed His foundations to be moved.

In this process of rebuilding, as you read through Ezra you will see there was great repentance and weeping accompanied by fasting. You will even find this in the book of Nehemiah which is a companion book of Ezra. At one point these books were combined. What I really want to highlight between the two books is the task of restoring the temple back to God's original design and how the gates were a key part of this restoration.

The Old Testament temple was a foreshadowing of the temples of the New Testament. Yes, I am talking about you and me!

Today God does not live in temples made by the hands of men, but in vessels of clay. Let me present several witnesses for this statement.

> **23 Therefore, the One whom you worship without knowing, Him I proclaim to you: 24 God, who made the world and everything in it, since He is Lord of heaven and earth, does not dwell in temples made with hands. 25 Nor is He worshiped with men's hands, as though He needed anything, since He gives to all life, breath, and all things.**
>
> **(Acts 17:23-25)**

1 Corinthians 6:18-20

> **18 Flee sexual immorality. Every sin that a man does is outside the body, but he who commits sexual immorality sins against his own body. 19 Or do you not know that <u>your body is the temple of the Holy Spirit who is in you</u>, whom you have from God, and you are not your own? 20 For you were bought at a**

price; therefore, glorify God in your body and in your spirit, which are God's.

The New Testament temple is you! The Holy Spirit now dwells in jars of clay- us **(2 Corinthians 4:7)**. Your body is the temple, and the gates must be established and stewarded in a manner which facilitates holiness. We think we know this, but it is apparent by the way we live our lives and what we permit to enter and exit our gates is in direct contradiction with the Word of the Living God. How we steward our temple also tells God how well we perceive this truth. We must have the same heart as in the days of Nehemiah and Ezra – **REPENT**, so the temple can be restored! Repentance does not mean I am sorry. The true definition of repentance is to think differently after hearing the truth. I can only think differently if I agree with whatever God says about the matter; this is what causes me to turn from any behavior contrary to His Word! This is true repentance.

As the temple of the Holy Spirit, we also have gates, and it is time we got back to guarding them. Gates allow access whether it be in our out. Take note, every gate that leads to something valuable has a gatekeeper. If you drive into an opulent neighborhood or go into any place which holds something of value, there is a gatekeeping system or a special code to gain access. Likewise, if we exit that same place, the guard will lift the gate, we may have an access pass on our vehicle or we can put in a code for the gate or door to open. What I want to really impress in your spirit is the word **ACCESS**! What you allow to come into the gates of your temple is the very thing which will come out of one of the main gates.

When I enter a high access area I do not enter by way of the gate as Sonya and come out as Teresa. No! I come back out at Sonya. What you allow to enter your gates is what will come back out. But here is the sobering truth about the outflow when dealing with the spiritual realm.; Seed multiplies in the realm of the spirit and creates a harvest. Seed does not come back as a seed. It comes back as the seed along with roots, leaves and FRUIT! We better believe a multiplied harvest is coming back from the seed which we allow to enter your gates. If we **intentionally** place ourselves in an unclean atmosphere, then we should be aware, an impure and unclean harvest is the outcome. On the contrary, when we yield our gates to what is pure, a pleasing and acceptable environment and harvest is the result. I pray this is the beginning of your awakening to prophetic purity!

CHAPTER 5

PURITY & THE GATES

As a prophets of the Lord, as prophetic people, it is our responsibility to guard the gates which lead to our heart. There are three main gates in particular I would like to address: the eye gate, ear gate and mouth gate. What we permit to enter our eyes and ears and will dramatically affect what comes out of our mouth. Protecting these gates is vital to flowing seamlessly with the Holy Spirit., seeing purely, hearing clearly, and speaking accurately.

Eye Gate

Our eyes are a critical gate to walking in purity. They are like having a built-in polaroid camera. Some of you may be too young to know what this is (laughing as I type this). Our eyes are constantly taking pictures all day long. Although we do not capture and retain everything, there are certain things which will command our attention more than others and leave a lasting impression upon our soul. To make this a little more impactful, please understand there are images we will focus on more than others which will create an indelible image on the screen of our imagination — our mind. There are some things we cannot unsee. Now let's look at the importance of the eye from a Scriptural standpoint.

Matthew 6:22-23

22 "The lamp of the body is the eye. If therefore your eye is good, your whole body will be full of light. 23 But if your eye is bad, your whole body will be full of darkness. If therefore the light that is in you is darkness, how great is that darkness!

Please answer this question and the ones to follow before you proceed through this book. What kind of light has been entering your temple? Is it the light of God or the light of darkness? Have you been setting your eyes on the right things and in the right places? If our *light* is darkness, or if darkness is what is flooding our soul, how do you think this will affect our prophetic flow? How do you think this will affect your prophetic perception? How do you think darkness filters through the soul? How will this affect your ability to see and deliver in purity? For this reason, we should be afraid to set our eyes on anything which highlights impurity to include sexual immorality, images of lewdness and perversity, coarse humor, death, macabre, and so forth. We should not watch TV shows and movies that come out because they are popular or have our favorite actor in them. We must ensure whatever we are watching does not compromise our eyes! So many have fallen into compromise in this area by saying, "Oh it had a biblical message in it." Baloney! The devil is very cunning. We must wake up and stop permitting the devil to lull us to sleep on his lap while he cuts our hair and weakens us, the same way Delilah did with Samson. Our strength is being robbed every time we permit impurity to enter our eye gate.

Whatever goes into your eye gate plants a seed in the womb of your mind. A baby is going to come forth from the seed. A birthing is going to happen sooner or later! We can fool ourselves to believe we are not affected by what we see or are mature enough to handle it, but this is not true. This kind of thought pattern is in direct conflict with the Word of God. We are either going to add images into our life that put out the light of the spiritual eye or make it brighter. The good thing is, we get to decide where we will permit our eyes to rest. I do not know about you, but I am not jeopardizing my place on the holy mountain of God because I want to be used mightily by the Holy Spirit!

Ear Gate

Another important spiritual gate in the temple is the ear gate. The Word of God cautions us to be careful how we hear. As prophets and prophetic people, we must do our best to remain in a position where what is going into our ears is wholesome and edifying. Again, what we allow to enter the ear gate will affect how we think and how we process what the Holy Spirit flows through us.

In Luke chapter 18 it says:

17 For nothing is secret that will not be revealed, nor anything hidden that will not be known and come to light. 18 Therefore take heed how you hear. For whoever has, to him more will be given; and whoever does not have, even what he seems to have will be taken from him (Luke 18:17-18).

Did you notice it says nothing is secret nor anything hidden? Everything comes to the light. Everything entering your ear gate will be revealed. What you have been hearing will come to the light through your conversation and behavior. The Holy Spirit needs you to be an active participant in guarding your ear gate to the best of your ability. By the way, you have permission to remove yourself from any atmosphere which does not accommodate this call to be separate. Most people will stay in the atmosphere because they do not want to offend people. If my removing myself offends a person into repentance, then so be it! I am sorry but I refuse to compromise. I have a right to protect my temple! The people of God, and especially prophets should be the first ones to extract themselves from an unholy or unwholesome atmosphere!

Mouth Gate

The mouth gate is greatly affected by what has passed through the ear and the eye gates. If you have not done a good job guarding your ear and eye gates, it will show up when the lever of the mouth gate is pulled back and your flow comes forth. What comes forth from this gate, is undeniable evidence of what has gone in. If being a prophet or being a prophetic person requires that we speak on behalf of the Lord, what manner of people should we be? How does one posture themselves when we come to the realization that we are in fact a mouthpiece for God? If we guard our gates, we also guard our heart.

> ***Keep your heart with all vigilance, for from it <u>flow</u> the springs of life (Proverbs 4:23).***

Guarding our gates will produce a pure life as well as a pure flow in the realm of the spirit. As we take our responsibility in these areas, we will see, hear, and speak from a place of purity and our soul will not taint what the Spirit of the Lord releases through us. When we guard the gates and keep our heart clean, we will function effectively with the Holy Spirit and many lives will be changed.

We will continue to move forward and investigate other areas which hinder our prophetic purity.

CHAPTER 6

LACK OF WASHING

By far, one of the most dangerous prophets is one who relies on the gift of God in them without ensuring the soul is properly washed on a daily basis by the Word. The Holy Spirit expects upon us to meditate on and study the Word to first cleanse us and then to properly handle what we hear or see in light of the Scripture. Daily washing with the water of the Word keeps us from venturing into error. I have personally witnessed prophets release a word that ended up taking on error because what came forth was no way validated by Scripture. I have often seen their emotions, their own understanding or perspective get intertwined with what came forth. They may have seen or heard something correctly but by the time it came out of their mouth it was tainted and skewed. A great man of God I know, once said, ***"The mind is the corruptor of the Word of God."*** Your soul needs to be washed and tutored properly by the Word to avoid passing it through a tainted or unclean filter and delivering the message in error.

Ephesians 5:25-27

25 Husbands, love your wives, just as Christ also loved the church and gave Himself for her, 26 that He might sanctify and <u>cleanse her with the washing of water by the word</u>, 27 that He might present her to Himself a glorious church, not having spot or wrinkle or any such thing, but that she should be holy and without blemish.

The Holy Spirit washes us through the Word as we peer into the His perfect Law of Liberty. Unfortunately, there are a lot of us who are not bathing every day! As you can imagine, it is difficult to cause glory or anything glorious to come forth from and unwashed or tainted vessel. We are being depended upon as prophets and prophetic people to take time and sit with the Holy Spirit to be sanctified and cleansed by the Word.

We should also be skillful with the Word and have a grasp on foundations. We need to know how to rightly divide the Word, or we will inflict great pain and division in the body of Christ. Prophets should spend a great deal of time STUDYING the Word because we are mouthpieces for God!

Be diligent to present yourself approved to God, a worker who does not need to be ashamed, rightly dividing the word of truth (2 Timothy 2:15).

Washed For Position

I need to add this disclaimer as well, every Prophet is not called to the office of a teacher. The Holy Spirit is the one who decides what gift a person is and operates in the body of Christ. As we read the Word, we are being washed to stay in a position of purity and function. Granted, we are all teachers to some degree but that does not make us Holy Ghost assigned teachers. There is great danger in stepping into an office you have not been placed in. As prophets, we may talk a lot or get incredible insight in Scripture; somehow, many think they are supposed to teach too. If you are not called to the office of a teacher, please stay out of that lane! There has been so much damage in the body of Christ because people have self-inserted themselves as teachers. Take a seat only where the Holy

Spirit has set you, otherwise you will find out you have not been invited to the table and it will cause embarrassment when a you are asked to pick up your things and leave!

A few years ago, I watched a documentary on a great prophet of the Lord who decided to step into the office of the teacher as well. Because he was not called to this area, he began to lead many astray. He ended up establishing a church and an ungodly movement erupted. To this day they are still holding fast to his erroneous teaching and waiting for him to be resurrected! Almost five years ago, I had a similar experience with a prophet close to me She was not content with where God had placed her and grasped for what God had not laid hold of for her. I am placed as a teacher in the body of Christ and to her, teaching looked more attractive and seemed as though more attention was being given in that area. This resulted in her releasing "spot" into the lives of many, and ultimately disrupted her divine destiny. It was a sad outcome for sure.

Please take this godly advice and stick with what God has called you to do. There is nothing wrong with being a Prophet of the Lord or being a prophetic person. This is a high calling of the

Lord. Just think of it, you get the privilege of being a spokesman for the Holy Spirit! What can be better than that?

CHAPTER 7

LOOK AT ME

Make no mistake about it, declaring what thus says the Lord will draw attention to us whether we want it or not. When people's lives are impacted by a prophetic Word from God, they tend to be drawn to the man instead of keeping their focus on God. As a prophet, or as prophetic people, the key to staying in a pure place, is making sure we are not using God's gift to command attention to ourselves. Nor should we ignore it when people try to insert us in His space.

We absolutely cannot permit people to make us their god or make us the replacement for the voice of God! Our only job is to release whatever the Holy Spirit has given us and then point them back to Jesus! We should NEVER allow ourselves to touch or intercept His glory! The flesh loves attention, but this kind of attention is costly. I do not believe it is intentional or starts out this way, but somehow some prophets of God begin to get puffed up or move in a vein of pride, because **"I said"** and it happened; or **"I prophesied,"** and it came to pass. Please remember, we own nothing God says, we are only a vessel to deliver His message!

James 4:6

But He gives more grace. Therefore He says, "God resists the proud, But gives grace to the humble."

I would like to paint a picture of pride on your canvas — your imagination. I was ministering a few years ago and a man came into the meeting who was so full of pride. Before he was pointed out to me by the Holy Spirit, I could feel its tangible presence in the room. The room felt full, but not of the presence of God. I had not noticed him until the Lord highlighted him during the meeting. I looked away from him and said, "There is a man here and your ego has literally inflated the room. You know who you are, and the Lord is giving you the opportunity to repent or to get up and leave now." He did neither one. I later found out he was a pastor. For some reason, the pride in him arose as I was moving in the Spirit prophetically and laying hands on the sick seeing them healed and made whole.

After aggressively binding up this devil we continued to minister and the atmosphere finally broke open. A few months later I received a call from a gentleman who attended the meeting. It turns out, the man of pride was a friend of his. He confirmed his identity with me. He confronted him as a friend, and said, "I believe she was talking about you in the meeting. The Holy Spirit is showing me it was you." I do not recall the meat of their conversation, but one thing I do know is he refused to repent. Unfortunately, the man of pride was a pastor who ended up losing his home, business, and ministry because of that night. He even ended up having to move in with his mom. Beloved, pride is a devil and loves attention! It was the downfall of Lucifer and has been the downfall of so many great women of God. It was not enough to have the music in him; He loved the attention and decided he wanted it all. He wanted the adoration and glory of God all to himself. He wanted to be God! We must avoid it at all cost.

In the book of Luke chapter 10, when the seventy returned from ministering and seeing great demonstrations of power, Jesus had to bring them back down to earth. He had to put the fire of pride out immediately because if it continues to burn, ruin is the result.

> ***17 Then the seventy returned with joy, saying, "Lord, even the demons are subject to us in Your name." 18 And He said to them, "I saw Satan fall like lightning from heaven. 19 Behold, I give you the authority to trample on serpents and scorpions, and over all the power of the enemy, and nothing shall by any means hurt you. 20 Nevertheless do not rejoice in this, that the spirits are subject to you, but rather rejoice because your names are written in heaven (Luke 10:17-20).***

The seventy were enthralled with the fact that the demons obeyed them and as a result, they saw many miracles. I can hear them now saying, "Look at us! We prophesied in your Name, released words of knowledge and devils were subject to US!" In this hour, Jesus is telling us the same thing He told the seventy on that day. He told them, and I paraphrase, "Oh that's great, but I saw Satan FALL from heaven like lightening!" He does not want us to get tied up in the attention of what "we did," because He saw Satan fall like lightening from heaven. He saw the effect of pride and wanted to let them know He had seen something even greater! On Jesus' behalf, let me bring you back down to earth and put the fire of pride out before it consumes you. Let me warn you about the deadly results of pride! Beloved, you will go down like lightening if you do not keep your distance from the glory of God! You will hit hard and fast if you adopt the "look at me" attitude or conversation.

It Is Not The Cup

Here is a valuable quote the Holy Spirit gave me one day when I was teaching; and I would love for you to put this on a sticky note and keep it before you. **<u>No one falls in love with the cup.</u>** Allow me to expand on this quote for a moment. When we are thirsty for a drink of water, do we stand there and marvel at the cup? Do we ignore what is in the cup and stop at the actual vessel, praising and adoring it, while never taking a drink? The vessel is not the proper place to focus one's attention when we are thirsty. If we did, we would never have our thirst quenched.! In like manner, do not let people fall in love with us. We are just the cup. What they are really after and attracted to is the fresh, pure quenching flow of the Holy Spirit that flows from our lives. When you remember you are the vessel, and point them back to Him, a greater level of anointing will be waiting for you and it will greatly aid in having a pure prophetic flow.

Chapter 8

I AM THE ONLY ONE/IT IS ALL MINE

This chapter is a continuation of the thread started in chapter 7. Somehow prophets and prophetic people have convinced themselves that they are thc **ONLY** ones declaring the Word of the Lord and tend to reject anything they are not hearing directly. Just because we are not hearing it does not mean God is not saying it! Prophetic companies carry a particular Word for the kingdom. Ultimately, all the pieces make a whole to fulfill the mandate of God for the hour. The truth of the matter is, you may be the only one in your circle of influence declaring a particular Word, but you are not the only one saying it in the body of Christ. For me personally, there have been only a few rare moments where I have been entrusted with a Word in which no one in my sphere of influence was speaking what I had heard from God. I can think of one right now that none of my counterparts are heralding. However, that does not mean I have ownership of the Word, nor do

I need to remind people that I am the one who released it for this decade, when others begin to come into concert with what the Holy Spirit has spoken from time past.

I want to remind you of something vital, the Holy Spirit is the prophet in you! We can speak nothing of truth without Him. We know nothing of spiritual substance without Him! Whatever I declare as thus says the Lord is exactly that, what the LORD has said, not what Sonya has said! When I see people who like to own the Word, I see someone who is looking for validation and who is saying this is my word because God gave it to me! The last time I checked my Bible it says in *Jeremiah 1:12* that God watches over His Word to perform it. Our job is not to watch it to point it back to ourselves. Our job is to release it and allow the Holy Spirit to perform it!

Lastly, I want to address the copyright prophets. This is another form or ownership. I have also noticed men and women of God who get a quote from the Holy Spirit and have the audacity to copyright it. Generally, when we copyright something it means I am the originator of it. How does one take the wisdom from the Holy Spirit and copyright it? Again, this is an attempt of ownership. Even as an author, although my books are copyrighted, I know the information will be used, taught, and quoted but I will never allow that to offend me because it is not my idea anyway. It belongs to God and He just happened to use me to speak or release it to His people.

How do we stay out of this area of impurity? We must learn how to eventually pull the plug or disconnect ourselves from the excitement and emotion that comes from God releasing a Word of God! Doing this will keep us out of a place of pride. If the Holy Spirit wants to have someone recall a word He had you release, then He will orchestrate it. Jesus quoted Old Testament prophets quite frequently during His teachings. So, let God be the one to retrace the word, not you. Self-validation is costly!

Chapter 9

IT IS NOT A WEAPON

I have often wondered how any man or woman of God could be bold enough to say they already know what is going on in someone's life, or that the Holy Spirit will show them what is going on whether they tell them or not. Being in the office of a prophet or being prophetic people does not give us a free pass to look into anyone's life at will! Being a prophet does not mean you can pull the covers back in a man or woman's life and uncover their flaws. Now, I realize the prophetic flow is not all uncovering flaws or exposing areas which need healing, but this is one of the main statements used as a weapon of threat and intimidation in the body of Christ when it comes to hidden faults in a person's life.

How is it so many leaders/prophets feel like everyone's laundry gets exposed except for theirs? How does one believe everybody's business can be exposed except for their own? A statement of such comes from a place of ignorance, error, impurity, and pride. It is also one which brings a "manipulated fear" into the lives of the people we are ministering to or are close to. A statement of such sends a subliminal message which places a man or woman of God in the place of the all-knowing, all-seeing God! I do not believe this is intentional with most, because they are merely repeating what they have heard someone else say. It is an example of passing on spiritual spot. The Holy Spirit will NEVER show everything about your life to anyone!

God will never expose your business unless you continue to ignore Him; It is only then that He will open your life up to someone who He believes is capable of pulling you out of the place of disobedience or obscurity. I want to caution you to steer clear of comments like this. Do not tell people around you, you already know, and God will show you anyway. Conversations like this are an invitation for the judgement of God because being a prophet or a prophetic people is not to be used as a weapon of control and manipulation.

A few of the purposes of the prophetic is to connect people back to God, to equip them through a Word from God, to touch them in an intimate way so they can know God has them on His mind, to give them wisdom and direction and to aid them in accomplishing their God designed destiny. What has happened is the uneducated in this area have gotten themselves stuck in the posture of an Old Testament prophet and see the function only as a means to pull back the covers of a person's life and expose them. This impure mindset must be purged from the body of Christ, like yesterday!

I am going to close out this chapter with a biblical example, where one of the most powerful prophets of the time – Elisha, could not see into the life of a woman who sought him after her child had died.

2 Kings 4:18-22 & 27

18 And the child grew. Now it happened one day that he went out to his father, to the reapers. 19 And he said to his father, "My head, my head!" So he said to a servant, "Carry him to his mother." 20 When he had taken him and brought him to his mother, he sat on her knees till noon, and then died. 21 And she went up and laid him on the bed of the man of God, shut the door upon him, and went out. 22 Then she called to her husband, and said, "Please send me one of the young men and one of the donkeys, that I may run to the man of God and come back."

27 Now when she came to the man of God at the hill, she caught him by the feet, but Gehazi came near to push her away. But the man of God said, "Let her alone; for her soul is in deep distress, and the Lord has <u>hidden it from me</u>, and has not told me."

You do understand what the word HIDDEN means don't you? It means to be veiled or concealed. Granted this is not a case of a hidden sin, but it does show that we will not be able to see everything in a person's life. Elisha, one of the most powerful prophets in What we need to do is posture in Scripture could not see into her life because the Holy Spirit had covered it. We need to posture ourselves the same way Elisha did; if God does not reveal it, we wait and let the person tell us what is on their heart. This will keep us out of error and ensure we walk in prophetic purity.

CHAPTER 10

THE NEED FOR MATURITY

A premature prophet can cause great injury when he/she releases something before its God ordained time. A prophet who cannot be quiet or hold a word until the time of release is a dangerous one! For this reason, we must be in a constant pursuit to master our mouth!

In **Psalm 143:3**, David cried out to God to get help him with his mouth

"Set a guard, O Lord, over my mouth; keep watch over the door of my lips."

Prophet of the Lord, prophetic people of God, this must be our heart's cry to God. Invite the Holy Spirit to help you put a seal on your lips, so you do not interrupt the process of His divine plan. We must have a fear of the Lord when it comes to prematurely releasing anything before its time! Just because you heard it does not mean it needs to be shared now or ever! The revelation or Word may need to be sealed up until a more appropriate time or just prayed over. Sometimes the Holy Spirit reveals just for intercessory intervention. It is possible that the event or outcome can be changed by God inspired prayer!

There are two examples I would like for you to look as it pertains to prophetic maturity.

> *"At that time Michael shall stand up, The great prince who stands watch over the sons of your people; And there shall be a time of trouble, Such as never was since there was a nation, Even to that time. And at that time your people shall be delivered, Every one who is found written in the book. 2 And many of those who sleep in the dust of the earth shall awake, Some to everlasting life, Some to shame and everlasting contempt. 3 Those who are wise shall shine Like the brightness of the firmament, And those who turn many to righteousness Like the stars forever and ever 4 "But you, Daniel, <u>shut up the words, and seal the book</u> until the time of the end; many shall run to and fro, and knowledge shall increase." (Daniel 12:1-4).*

In the example above, the Spirit of God told Daniel to shut up the revelation or keep it a secret.

What is funny is some folks cannot keep a secret for ten minutes; They must tell someone. This is a sure sign of immaturity, which if left unchecked or cured, makes the individual untrustworthy and potentially dangerous! This is where impurity comes in. Immaturity can lead to impurity! The Holy Spirit also told Daniel to "**seal the book**." He was told to lock up the written revelation, so it could not be opened before its time.

Let's also look in the book of Revelation.

I saw still another mighty angel coming down from heaven, clothed with a cloud. And a rainbow was on his head, his face was like the sun, and his feet like pillars of fire. 2 He had a little book open in his hand. And he set his right foot on the sea and his left foot on the land, 3 and cried with a loud voice, as when a lion roars. When he cried out, seven thunders uttered their voices. 4 Now when the seven thunders uttered their voices, I was about to write; but I heard a voice from heaven saying to me, "<u>Seal up the things which the seven thunders uttered,</u> and <u>do not write them.</u>" (Revelation 10:1-4)

In this case, we see John the revelator, a great prophet of the Lord, who was given great revelation but was told to seal it and do not write it. I must point out, even in this case, we have never heard what the angel shared with John, but it shall come forth in its set and ordained time! If we want to be recipients of the secret things of God and be used by Him mightily; we must be adamant about saying only what we are told to say, revealing only those things the Holy Spirit has approved and being silent and sealing up what He has told you to shut.

You Have Control

As a sub to this chapter, we must understand, we are in control. The Holy Spirit will not make us say or not say anything. We decide to cooperate and submit to Him. For example, when you are publicly flowing with the Holy Spirit, there are moments where the He will share something with you but you must put the brakes on and whisper it to the person, hold it for a private sitting with the individual or say nothing until the time or release. I cannot tell you how many people have been embarrassed and injured by prophets and prophetic people because they did not take time to operate with the Spirit and see if what they heard was something which needed to be said publicly or privately. Heaven help us if we do not mature in this area! Countless lives have been rattled and destinies misaligned because someone did not know when to shut their mouth. Then, after injury or a premature release of a Word results, I have heard prophets and prophetic folks say, "I could not hold it. It was burning in me!" My friend, this is not true. We are very much in control of what comes forth. What I find interesting is that some prophets/prophetic people are far more eager to release correction and insight more than they are a Word which pushes someone into their correct destiny. It is then that they suddenly want to make sure they have heard from God. Look at this text in Corinthians.

1 Corinthians 14: 29-33

29 Let two or three prophets speak, and let the others judge. 30 But if anything is revealed to another who sits by, let the first keep silent. 31 For you can all prophesy one by one, that all may learn and all may be encouraged. 32 And the <u>spirits of the prophets are subject to the prophets</u>. 33 For God is not

the author of confusion but of peace, as in all the churches of the saints.

The Prophetic gift of utterance is not controlled by the Holy Spirit. We are the ones who release or shut up the word He gives us. Therefore, it is imperative to learn how to work with Him and take time to hear clearly before we declare what we believe He is saying or showing us. We must learn to be orderly as well. With greater submission comes greater trust. With greater submission comes greater ability to operate in the prophetic office or gift. With greater submission comes a greater MATURITY which leads to prophetic PURITY!

Chapter 11

NOT SPEAKING THE TRUTH IN LOVE

Someone once made a statement to me which has never left me and has become the framework for much of what the Holy Spirit has uncovered during times of prayer in public ministry. The statement is such, **"God reveals to redeem."** This statement is one of the foundations for keeping me in a place of love, in times when the Holy Spirit reveals something sinful or negative about the life of an individual. **<u>I believe the greatest impurity of them all is to operate in the gifts of God outside of the love of God</u>**. The revealing of a hidden sin or flaw does not cause me to view a person differently or turn my nose up at them. No, I know it is only being done because God would really like to bring them out of darkness into His marvelous light. My response may be one to pray for them or reach out and share what the Lord has shown me. If I am compelled by the Spirit to reach out to the individual, I must also be prepared to minister to them through the Word of God. This will not only bring repentance but comfort, even in correction.

Ephesians 4 is clear on what our heart's posture should be

11 And He Himself gave some to be apostles, some prophets, some evangelists, and some pastors and teachers, 12 for the equipping of the saints for the work of ministry, for the edifying of the body of Christ, 13 till we all come to the unity of the faith and of the knowledge of the Son of God, to a perfect man, to the measure of the stature of the fullness of Christ; 14 that we should no longer be children, tossed to and fro and carried about with every wind of doctrine, by the trickery of men, in the cunning craftiness of deceitful plotting, 15 <u>but, speaking the truth in love, may grow up in all things into Him who is the head—Christ— 16 from whom the whole body, joined and knit together by what every joint supplies, according to the effective working by which every part does its share, causes growth of the body for the edifying of itself in love.</u>

(Ephesians 4:11-16)

When we do not speak the truth in love, it hinders the growth of the individual, as well as the growth of the body of Christ. From a natural standpoint, an injured joint affects the whole body. It affects our effectiveness, it affects movement, production, and efficiency. This is also the case from a spiritual standpoint. Every joint must be in place to properly supply the body of Christ and ensure we are effective for the kingdom. This is how we will grow purely and properly.

Even when a word is correcting, we must not deliver it through the flesh in a way which makes the person feel exposed, hurt, or embarrassed. Some people take delight in "reading people's mail," as if they have an upper hand and want to pull back the covers to show everyone that they know the sin or hidden areas of the person's life. They forget that this is an opportunity for the Holy Spirit, by way of His grace and love, to minister and cause the individual come back into a place of agreement with God! The Lord will hold us accountable for injuring His people. Therefore, we need to be very careful in intercepting our soul's desire to catch the Word and deliver it in anger, cynicism or in any impure manner.

2 Peter 3:8-9 is a Scripture you will want to keep before you. It is the heart of the Father and should be the heart of every prophet and every prophetic person.

> *8 But, beloved, do not forget this one thing, that with the Lord one day is as a thousand years, and a thousand years as one day. 9 <u>The Lord is not slack concerning His promise, as some count slackness, but is longsuffering toward us, not willing that any should perish but that all should come to repentance.</u>*

Please remember, repentance is always the outcome when a Word from the Lord finds someone in a place outside of the will of God or struggling in an area. One of the key areas the Holy Spirit wants to clean us up in is how we deliver His truth! Beloved when we each speak the truth in love, the entire body of Christ will benefit. We will see a healthy body which is equipped, whole and functioning **IN** the love of Christ and you will have had a great part in accomplishing His desire!

ABOUT THE AUTHOR

Apostle Sonya L. Thompson of ARISE Ministries International is called as a teacher to the body of Christ to; **"Train, Educate and Advise through the Gospel with Simplicity and Purity."** She holds a Bachelor of Science in the field of Business Administration, a Master of Arts in Biblical Leadership and a Doctorate in Biblical Finances. She is an entrepreneur, mentor and spiritual mother. Apostle Thompson was ordained as a Pastor by world renowned minister of the gospel, Dr. Nasir Siddiki and affirmed as an Apostle, by Apostle Jerry D. Owens of Joshua Generation Outreach Church.

She is driven to introduce people to the Living God; To teach the Living word; To equip & edify the body of Christ for the work of ministry; To lead others to encounter the abiding presence of God in a way which will forever change their lives; To see an awakening that leads to Revival!

OTHER BOOKS BY APOSTLE SONYA L. THOMPSON

Break Out of Poverty Into Financial Abundance

Business By The Bible

Declare Yourself Wealthy

**Faith To Build (Free e-Book)*

**Fully Functional Faith (Free e-Book)*

Glory Walkers Revealed

He Restores My Soul

**Hem of His Garment (free e-Book)*

**Seed Conversations (Free e-Book)*

Seeds of Prosperity For A Financial Revolution

All books available on amazon or visit.
https://ariseapostolic.com
ariseministriesintl.com

*Free e-book available on website

Social Media Platforms:

FB: Ariseministriesintl

Podcast: http://www.voiceofreasonpodcast.com

Intsagram: ariseministriesinternational

To book Dr. Thompson send booking requests to: Info@ariseministriesintl.com